SAMUEL DANIEL
A DEFENCE OF RYME (1603)
THOMAS CAMPION
OBSERVATIONS IN THE ART OF ENGLISH POESIE (1602)

ELIZABETHAN AND JACOBEAN QUARTOS

ELIZABETHAN AND JACOBEAN QUARTOS
EDITED BY G. B. HARRISON

SAMUEL DANIEL
A DEFENCE OF RYME
Against a Pamphlet entituled:
Obseruations in the Art of English Poesie
1603

THOMAS CAMPION
OBSERVATIONS IN THE
ART OF ENGLISH POESIE
1602

BARNES & NOBLE, Inc.
New York, New York

This edition published in 1966
by Barnes & Noble, Inc.
is reproduced from the series
BODLEY HEAD QUARTOS
published by
John Lane The Bodley Head Ltd., London
between 1922 and 1926

Printed in the United States of America

INTRODUCTION

SAMUEL DANIEL'S *Defence of Ryme* and Thomas Campion's *Obseruations in the Art of English Poesie*, which it answered, both have a permanent importance in the history of English criticism. The *Obseruations* is the last and best attempt in Elizabethan times to persuade English poets to use classical metres. There was nothing very new in the proposal. Almost a generation earlier, Gabriel Harvey had prided himself on being the Inventor of the English hexameter, and he had pressed his views on Spenser. Campion, however, was mainly concerned with lyrical poetry: he would have nothing to do with the English hexameter, which had 'bene oftentimes attempted in our English toong, but with passing pitifull sucesse: and no wonder, seeing it is an attempt altogether against the nature of our language'. His attitude, at first sight, is the more surprising because in the generation which had followed the *Shepheardes Calender* (1579), English poets had produced many incomparable lyrics, to

which Campion himself had made notable contri-
bution in the *Booke of Ayres* which he had published
in collaboration with his friend the musician,
Philip Rosseter, in 1601.

But Campion was primarily a classical scholar
and had first made his reputation with his Latin
Poemata (printed in 1595). His real objection to
English rhymed verse was that it was so vulgar
and easy, fit only for these 'lack-learning times';
the truly ingenious wit required something
complex to raise his mind 'to a more high and
lofty conceit.' Accordingly he proceeds to point
the harder way by compiling a set of instructions
for the use of classical metres in the English tongue.
The Obseruations in the Art of English Poesie, in
short, is an experiment, and an experiment which
failed; for Campion convinced no one, not even
himself. When next he published English poetry,
he returned to the 'vulgar and vnarteficiall custome
of riming'. The *Obseruations*, however, contains
many shrewd remarks on English quantity made
by one who was a skilled musician as well as an able
poet; above all it called forth *The Defence of Ryme*,
of which Professor Saintsbury writes as follows:

'Not easily shall we find, either in Elizabethan
times or in any other, a happier combination of

solid good sense with eager poetic sentiment, of sound scholarship with wide-glancing intelligence, than in this little tractate of some thirty or forty ordinary pages, which dispelled the delusions of two generations, and made the poetical fortune of England sure.'[1]

The tone of Daniel's reply to Campion is dignified and courteous, very different from the abusive 'flytings' in which the more needy pamphleteers of the time indulged. For the debate was private: both poets appealed to the select literary set in which they moved.

The *Defence of Ryme* was published in 1603, being bound up with Daniel's *Panegyrike Congratulatorie to King James*. Two editions were published in that year, a folio for presentation and private circulation, and a quarto for the public. Our text has been reprinted from the folio edition.

G. B. HARRISON

King's College,
University of London.

---

[1] *History of Criticism*, ii, 189.

Obseruations in the
Art of English Poesie
1602

OBSERVATIONS
in the Art of English Poesie.

By *Thomas Campion*.

Wherein it is demonstra-
tiuely prooued, and by example
confirmed, that the English toong
will receiue eight seuerall kinds of num-
bers, proper to it selfe, which are all
in this booke set forth, and were
neuer before this time by any
man attempted.

Printed at London by RICHARD FIELD
for *Andrew Wise*. 1602.

Note

THE ORIGINAL of this text is in the British Museum (8vo. 1076. b. 18). The text (not the *Epistle*) is reprinted page for page and line for line. A list of the misprints which have been corrected will be found on page 44.

G. B. H.

ꝑ To the Right Noble and

worthily honourd, the Lord
Buckhurst, Lord high Trea-
surer of England.

N two things (right honorable)
it is generally agreed that man
excels all other creatures, in
reason, and speech: and in them
by how much one man surpas-
seth an other, by so much the
neerer he aspires to a celestiall essence.

Poesy in all kind of speaking is the / [A3
chiefe beginner, and maintayner of eloquence,
not only helping the eare with the acquaintance of sweet numbers, but also raysing the
minde to a more high and lofty conceite. For
this end haue I studyed to induce a true
forme of versefying into our language: for the
vulgar and vnarteficiall custome of riming
hath I know deter'd many excellent wits from
the exercise of English Poesy. The obseruations which I haue gathered for this purpose,

I humbly present to your Lordship, as to the noblest iudge of Poesy, and the most honorable protector of all industrious learning; which if your Honour shall vouchsafe / [A3^v to receiue, who both in your publick, and priuate Poemes haue so deuinely crowned your fame, what man will dare to repine? or not striue to imitate them? VVherefore with all humility I subiect my selfe and them to your gratious fauour, beseeching you in the noblenes of your mind to take in worth so simple a present, which by some worke drawne from my more serious studies, I will hereafter endeuour to excuse.

Your Lordships humbly deuoted
THOMAS CAMPION.

[A4

then sem'briefes) so in a verse the numeration of the sillables is not so much to be obserued, as their waite, and due proportion. In ioyning of words to harmony there is nothing more offensiue to the eare then to place a long sillable with a short note, or a short sillable with a long note, though in the last the vowell often beares it out. The wo___ ___ made by Simmetry and proportio___ ___ ___

resp___ ___ ___ M___ ___

The Writer to his
Booke.

WHether thus hasts my little booke so fast?
* To Paules Churchyard; what in those cels to stād,*
With one leafe like a riders cloke put vp
To catch a termer? or lye mustie there
With rimes a terme set out, or two before?
Some will redeeme me; fewe; yes, reade me too;
Fewer; nay loue me; now thou dot'st I see;
Will not our English Athens *arte defend?*
Perhaps; will lofty courtly wits not ayme
Still at perfection? If I graunt? I flye;
Whether? to Pawles; Alas poore booke I rue
Thy rash selfe-loue, goe spread thy pap'ry wings,
Thy lightnes can not helpe, or hurt my fame.

℘ Obser-

℘ Obseruations in the Art
of English Poesy, by *Thomas*
Campion.

The first Chapter, intreating of numbers
in generall.

℘ Here is no writing too breefe, that
        ...thout obscuritie comprehends

Epistolæ obscurorum virorum, may sufficiently testi-
fie. In those lack-learning times, and in barbarized
Italy, began that vulgar and easie kind of Poesie
which is now in vse throughout most parts of
Christendome, which we abusiuely call Rime, and
Meeter, of *Rithmus* and *Metrum*, of which I will
now discourse.

The second Chapter, declaring the vnaptnesse of Rime in Poesie.

I Am not ignorant that whosoeuer shall by way
of reprehension examine the imperfections of
Rime, must encounter with many glorious ene-
mies, and those very expert, and ready at their
weapon, that can if neede be extempore (as they
say) rime a man to death. Besides there is growne
a kind of prescription in the vse of Rime, to fore-
stall the right of true numbers, as also the consent
of many nations, against all which it may seeme a
thing almost impossible, and vaine to contend.
All this and more can not yet deterre me from a
lawful defence of perfection, or make me any whit
the sooner adheare to that which is lame and vn-
beseeming. For custome I alleage, that ill vses are

to be abolisht, and that things naturally imperfect
can not be perfected by vse. Old customes, if they
be better, why should they not be recald, as the yet
florishing custome of numerous poesy vsed among
the *Romanes* and *Grecians:* But the vnaptnes of
our toongs, and the difficultie of imitation dishar-
tens vs; againe the facilitie & popularitie of Rime
creates as many Poets, as a hot sommer flies. But
let me now examine the nature of that which we
call Rime. By Rime is vnderstoode that which
ends in the like sound, so that verses in such maner
composed, yeeld but a continual repetition of that
Rhetoricall figure which we tearme *similiter desi-
nentia*, and that being but *figura verbi*, ought (as
Tully and all other Rhetoritians haue iudicially
obseru'd) sparingly to be vsd, least it should offend
the eare with tedious affectation. Such was that
absurd following of the letter amõgst our English
so much of late affected, but now hist out of Paules
Churchyard: which foolish figuratiue repetition
crept also into the Latine toong, as it is manifest in
the booke of Ps cald *prælia porcorum*, and an o-
ther pamphlet all of Fs, which I haue seene im-
printed; but I will leaue these follies to their owne
ruine, and returne to the matter intended. The
                                                    eare

eare is a rationall sence, and a chiefe iudge of proportion, but in our kind of riming what proportion is there kept, where there remaines such a
confusd inequalitie of sillables? *Iambick* and *Tro-*
chaick feete which are opposd by nature, are by all
Rimers confounded, nay oftentimes they place in
stead of an *Iambick* the foote *Pyrrychius*, consisting
of two short sillables, curtalling their verse, which
they supply in reading with a ridiculous, and vnapt
drawing of their speech. As for example:

　　Was it my desteny, or dismall chaunce?

In this verse the two last sillables of the word, *De-*
steny, being both short, and standing for a whole
foote in the verse, cause the line to fall out shorter
then it ought by nature. The like impure errors
haue in time of rudenesse bene vsed in the Latine
toong, as the *Carmina prouerbialia* can witnesse,
and many other such reuerend bables. But the
noble *Grecians* and *Romaines* whose skilfull monuments outliue barbarisme, tyed themselues to the
strict obseruation of poeticall numbers, so aban-
doning the childish titillation of riming, that it
was imputed a great error to *Ouid* for setting forth
this one riming verse,

　　Quot cælum stellas tot habet tua Roma puellas.

For the establishing of this argument, what better
confirmation can be had, then that of Sir *Thomas
Moore* in his booke of Epigrams, where he makes
two sundry Epitaphs vpon the death of a singing
man at *Westminster*, the one in learned numbers
and dislik't, the other in rude rime and highly ex-
told: so that he concludes, *tales lactucas talia labra
petunt*, like lips, like lettuce. But there is yet another fault in Rime altogether intollerable, which is,
that it inforceth a man oftentimes to abiure his
matter, and extend a short conceit beyond all
bounds of arte: for in *Quatorzens* me thinks the
Poet handles his subiect as tyrannically as *Procru-
stes* the thiefe his prisoners, whom when he had
taken, he vsed to cast vpon a bed, which if they
were too short to fill, he would stretch thē longer,
if too long, he would cut them shorter. Bring before me now any the most selfe-lou'd Rimer, & let
me see if without blushing he be able to reade his
lame halting rimes. Is there not a curse of Nature
laid vpon such rude Poesie, when the Writer is
himself asham'd of it, and the hearers in contempt
call it Riming and Ballating? What Deuine in his
Sermon, or graue Counseller in his Oration will
alleage the testimonie of a rime? But the deuinity
of

of the *Romaines* and *Gretians* was all written in verse: and *Aristotle*, *Galene*, and the bookes of all the excellent Philosophers are full of the testimonies of the old Poets. By them was laid the foundation of all humane wisedome, and from them the knowledge of all antiquitie is deriued. I will propound but one question, and so conclude this point. If the *Italians*, *Frenchmen* and *Spanyards*, that with commendation haue written in Rime, were demaunded whether they had rather the bookes they haue publisht (if their toong would beare it) should remaine as they are in Rime, or be translated into the auncient numbers of the *Greekes* and *Romaines*, would they not answere into numbers? What honour were it then for our English language to be the first that after so many yeares of barbarisme could second the perfection of the industrious *Greekes* and *Romaines?* which how it may be effected I will now proceede to demonstrate.

The third Chapter: of our English numbers in generall.

THere are but three feete, which generally distinguish the Greeke and Latine verses, the

Dactil consisting of one long sillable and two short, as *vīuĕrĕ* the *Trochy*, of one long and one short, as *vītă*, and the *Iambick* of one short and one long, as *ămōr*. The *Spondee* of two long, the *Tribrach* of three short, the *Anapæstick* of two short and a long, are but as seruants to the first. Diuers other feete I know are by the Grammarians cited, but to little purpose. The *Heroical* verse that is distinguisht by the *Dactile*, hath bene oftentimes attempted in our English toong, but with passing pitifull successe: and no wonder, seeing it is an attempt altogether against the nature of our language. For both the concurse of our monasillables make our verses vnapt to slide, and also if we examine our polysillables, we shall finde few of them by reason of their heauinesse, willing to serue in place of a *Dactile*. Thence it is, that the writers of English heroicks do so often repeate *Amyntas, Olympus, Auernus, Erinnis,* and such like borrowed words, to supply the defect of our hardly intreated *Dactile*. I could in this place set downe many ridiculous kinds of *Dactils* which they vse, but that it is not my purpose here to incite men to laughter. If we therefore reiect the *Dactil* as vnfit for our vse (which of necessity we are enforst to do) there

remayne

remayne only the *Iambick* foote, of which the
Iambick verse is fram'd, and the *Trochee*, frõ which
the *Trochaick* numbers haue their originall. Let vs
now then examine the property of these two feete,
and try if they consent with the nature of our English sillables. And first for the *Iambicks*, they fall
out so naturally in our toong, that if we examine
our owne writers, we shall find they vnawares hit
oftentimes vpon the true *Iambick* numbers, but alwayes ayme at them as far as their eare without the
guidance of arte can attaine vnto, as it shall hereafter more euidently appeare. The *Trochaick* foote
which is but an *Iambick* turn'd ouer and ouer, must
of force in like manner accord in proportion with
our Brittish sillables, and so produce an English
Trochaicall verse. Then hauing these two princi-
pall kinds of verses, we may easily out of them de-
riue other formés, as the Latines and Greekes before vs haue done, whereof I will make plaine demonstration, beginning at the *Iambick* verse.

The fourth Chapter, of the Iambick verse.

I Haue obserued, and so may any one that is either practis'd in singing, or hath a naturall eare
B

able to time a song, that the Latine verses of sixe
feete, as the *Heroick* and *Iambick*, or of fiue feete,
as the *Trochaick* are in nature all of the same
length of sound with our English verses of fiue
feete; for either of them being tim'd with the hand
quinque perficiunt tempora, they fill vp the quantity
(as it were) of fiue sem'briefs, as for example, if any
man will proue to time these verses with his hand.

A pure *Iambick*.
Suis & ipsa Roma viribus ruit.
A licentiate *Iambick*.
Ducunt volentes fata, nolentes trahunt.
An *Heroick* verse.
Tytere tu patulæ recubans sub tegmine fagi.
A *Trochaick* verse.
Nox est perpetua vna dormienda.
English *Iambicks* pure.
The more secure, the more the stroke we feele
Of vnpreuented harms; so gloomy stormes
Appeare the sterner if the day be cleere.
Th'English *Iambick* licentiate.
Harke how these winds do murmur at thy flight.
The English *Trochee*.
Still where Enuy leaues, remorse doth enter.

The

The cause why these verses differing in feete yeeld the same length of sound, is by reason of some rests which either the necessity of the numbers, or the heauines of the sillables do beget. For we find in musick, that oftentimes the straines of a song can not be reduct to true number without some rests prefixt in the beginning and middle, as also at the close if need requires. Besides, our English monasillables enforce many breathings which no doubt greatly lengthen a verse, so that it is no wonder if for these reasons our English verses of fiue feete hold pace with the *Latines* of sixe. The pure *Iambick* in English needes small demonstration, because it consists simply of *Iambick* feete, but our *Iambick licentiate* offers it selfe to a farther consideration; for in the third and fift place we must of force hold the *Iambick* foote, in the first, second, and fourth place we may vse a *Spondee* or *Iambick* and sometime a *Tribrack* or *Dactile*, but rarely an *Anapestick* foote, and that in the second or fourth place. But why an *Iambick* in the third place? I answere, that the forepart of the verse may the gentlier slide into his *Dimeter*, as for example sake deuide this verse: *Harke how these winds do murmure at thy flight. Harke how these winds*, there the

B 2

voice naturally affects a rest, then *murmur at thy flight*, that is of it selfe a perfect number, as I will declare in the next Chapter, and therefore the other odde sillable betweene thẽ ought to be short, least the verse should hang too much betweene the naturall pause of the verse, and the *Dimeter* following, the which *Dimeter* though it be naturally *Trochaical*, yet it seemes to haue his originall out of the *Iambick* verse. But the better to confirme and expresse these rules, I will set downe a short Poeme in *Licentiate Iambicks*, which may giue more light to them that shall hereafter imitate these numbers.

> *Goe numbers boldly passe, stay not for ayde*
> *Of shifting rime, that easie flatterer*
> *Whose witchcraft can the ruder eares beguile;*
> *Let your smooth feete enur'd to purer arte*
> *True measures tread; what if your pace be slow?*
> *And hops not like the Grecian elegies?*
> *It is yet gracefull, and well fits the state*
> *Of words ill-breathed, and not shap't to runne:*
> *Goe then, but slowly till your steps be firme,*
> *Tell them that pitty, or peruersely skorne*
> *Poore English Poesie as the slaue to rime,*
> *You are those loftie numbers that reuiue*

Triumphs

Triumphs of Princes, and sterne tragedies:
And learne henceforth t'attend those happy sprights
Whose bounding fury, height, and waight affects,
Assist their labour, and sit close to them,
Neuer to part away till for desert
Their browes with great Apollos *bayes are hid.*
He first taught number, and true harmonye,
Nor is the lawrell his for rime bequeath'd,
Call him with numerous accents paisd by arte
He'le turne his glory from the sunny clymes,
The North-bred wits alone to patronise.
Let France their Bartas, *Italy* Tasso *prayse,*
Phæbus *shuns none, but in their flight from him.*

Though as I said before, the naturall breathing
place of our English *Iambick* verse is in the last
sillable of the second foote, as our *Trochy* after the
manner of the Latine *Heroick* and *Iambick* rests
naturally in the first of the third foote: yet no man
is tyed altogether to obserue this rule, but he may
alter it, after the iudgement of his eare, which
Poets, Orators, and Musitions of all men ought to
haue most excellent. Againe, though I said perem-
torily before, that the third, and fift place of our licentiate *Iambick* must alwayes hold an *Iambick*
foote, yet I will shew you example in both places

where a *Tribrack* may be very formally taken, and
first in the third place,

Some trade in Barbary, *some in* Turky *trade.*

An other example.

Men that do fall to misery, quickly fall.

If you doubt whether the first of misery be naturally short or no, you may iudge it by the easie sli-
ding of these two verses following:

The first.

Whome misery can not alter, time deuours.

The second.

What more vnhappy life, what misery more?

Example of the *Tribrack* in the fift place, as you
may perceiue in the last foote of the fift verse.

Some from the starry throne his fame deriues,
Some from the mynes beneath, from trees, or herbs,
Each hath his glory, each his sundry gift,
Renown'd in eu'ry art there liues not any.

To proceede farther, I see no reason why the English *Iambick* in his first place may not as well bor-
row a foote of the *Trochy,* as our *Trochy* or the Latine *Hendicasillable* may in the like case make bold
with the *Iambick:* but it must be done euer with
this caueat, which is, that a *Sponde, Dactile* or *Tribrack* do supply the next place: for an *Iambick* beginning

ginning with a single short sillable, and the other ending before with the like, would too much drinke vp the verse if they came immediatly together.

The example of the *Sponde* after
the *Trochy*.
As the faire sonne the lightsome heau'n adorns.
The example of the *Dactil*.
Noble, ingenious, and discreetly wise.
The example of the *Tribrack*.
Beawty to ielosie brings ioy, sorrow, feare.

Though I haue set downe these second licenses as good and ayreable enough, yet for the most part my first rules are generall.

These are those numbers which Nature in our English destinates to the Tragick, and Heroik Poeme: for the subiect of them both being all one, I see no impediment why one verse may not serue for them both, as it appeares more plainely in the old comparison of the two Greeke writers, when they say, *Homerus est Sophocles heroicus*, and againe, *Sophocles est Homerus tragicus*, intimating that both *Sophocles* and *Homer* are the same in height and subiect, and differ onely in the kinde of their numbers.

B 4

The *Iambick* verse in like manner being yet made a little more licentiate, that it may thereby the neerer imitate our common talke, will excellently serue for Comedies, and then may we vse a *Sponde* in the fift place, and in the third place any foote except a *Trochy*, which neuer enters into our *Iambick* verse, but in the first place, and then with his caueat of the other feete which must of necessitie follow.

The fift Chapter, of the Iambick Dimeter, or English march.

THe *Dimeter* (so called in the former Chapter) I intend next of all to handle, because it seems to be a part of the *Iambick* which is our most naturall and auncient English verse. We may terme this our English march, because the verse answers our warlick forme of march in similitude of number. But call it what you please, for I will not wrangle about names, only intending to set down the nature of it and true structure. It consists of two feete and one odde sillable. The first foote may be made either a *Trochy*, or a *Spondee*, or an *Iambick* at the pleasure of the composer, though

most

most naturally that place affects a *Trochy* or *Spondee*; yet by the example of *Catullus* in his *Hendicasillables*, I adde in the first place sometimes an *Iambick* foote. In the second place, we must euer insert a *Trochy* or *Tribrack*, and so leaue the last sillable (as in the end of a verse it is alwaies held) common. Of this kinde I will subscribe three examples, the first being a peece of a *Chorus* in a Tragedy.

> *Rauing warre begot*
> *In the thirstye sands*
> *Of the* Lybian *Iles*
> *Wasts our emptye fields,*
> *What the greedye rage*
> *Of fell wintrye stormes,*
> *Could not turne to spoile,*
> *Fierce* Bellona *now*
> *Hath laid desolate,*
> *Voyd of fruit, or hope.*
> *Th'eger thriftye hinde*
> *Whose rude toyle reuiu'd*
> *Our skie-blasted earth*
> *Himselfe is but earth,*
> *Left a skorne to fate*
> *Through seditious armes:*

F

And that soile, aliue
Which he duly nurst,
Which him duly fed,
Dead his body feeds:
Yet not all the glebe
His tuffe hands manur'd
Now one turfe affords
His poore funerall.
Thus still needy liues,
Thus still needy dyes
Th'vnknowne multitude.

An example *Lyrical.*

Greatest in thy wars,
Greater in thy peace
Dread Elizabeth;
Our muse only Truth
Figments can not vse
Thy ritch name to deck
That it selfe adornes:
But should now this age
Let all poesye fayne,
Fayning poesy could
Nothing faine at all
Worthy halfe thy fame.

An

An example *Epigram-
micall.*

*Kind in euery kinde
This deare Ned resolue,
Neuer of thy prayse
Be too prodigall;
He that prayseth all
Can praise truly none.*

*The sixt Chapter, of the English
Trochaick verse.*

NExt in course to be intreated of is the English
Trochaick, being a verse simple, and of it selfe
depending. It consists, as the Latine *Trochaick* of
fiue feete, the first whereof may be a *Trochy,* a *Spondee,* or an *Iambick,* the other foure of necessity all
Trochyes, still holding this rule authenticall, that
the last sillable of a verse is alwayes common. The
spirit of this verse most of all delights in *Epigrams,*
but it may be diuersly vsed, as shall hereafter be de-
clared. I haue written diuers light Poems in this
kinde, which for the better satisfaction of the reader, I thought conuenient here in way of example
to publish. In which though sometimes vnder a

knowne name I haue shadowed a fain'd conceit, yet is it done without reference, or offence to any person, and only to make the stile appeare the more English.

The first *Epigramme*.

Lockly spits apace, the rhewme he cals it,
But no drop (though often vrgd) he straineth
From his thirstie iawes, yet all the morning,
And all day he spits, in eu'ry corner,
At his meales he spits, at eu'ry meeting,
At the barre he spits before the Fathers,
In the Court he spits before the Graces,
In the Church he spits, thus all prophaning
With that rude disease, that empty spitting:
Yet no cost he spares, he sees the Doctors,
Keepes a strickt diet, precisely vseth
Drinks and bathes drying, yet all preuailes not.
'Tis not China (Lockly) Salsa Guacum,
Nor dry Sassafras *can helpe, or ease thee;*
'Tis no humor hurts, it is thy humor.

The second *Epigramme*.

Cease fond wretch to loue so oft deluded,

Still

Still made ritch with hopes, still vnrelieued,
Now fly her delaies; she that debateth
Feeles not true desire, he that deferred
Others times attends, his owne betrayeth:
Learne t'affect thy selfe, thy cheekes deformed
With pale care reuiue by timely pleasure,
Or with skarlet heate them, or by paintings
Make thee louely, for such arte she vseth
Whome in vayne so long thy folly loued.

The third *Epigramme.*

Kate *can fancy only berdles husbands,*
Thats the cause she shakes off eu'ry suter,
Thats the cause she liues so stale a virgin,
For before her heart can heate her answer,
Her smooth youths she finds all hugely berded.

The fourth *Epigramme.*

All in sattin Oteny *will be suted,*
Beaten sattin (as by chaunce he cals it)
Oteny *sure will haue the bastinado.*

The fift *Epigramme.*

Tosts as snakes or as the mortall Henbane

Hunks *detests when huffcap ale he tipples,*
Yet the bread he graunts the fumes abateth:
Therefore apt in ale, true, and he graunts it,
But it drinks vp ale, that Hunks *detesteth.*

The sixt *Epigramme.*

What though Harry *braggs, let him be noble,*
Noble Harry *hath not halfe a noble.*

The seauenth *Epigramme.*

Phæbe *all the rights* Elisa *claymeth,*
Mighty riuall, in this only diff'ring
That shees only true, thou only fayned.

The eight *Epigramme.*

Barnzy *stiffly vowes that hees no Cuckold,*
Yet the vulgar eu'ry where salutes him
With strange signes of hornes, from eu'ry corner,
Wheresoere he commes a sundry Cucco
Still frequents his eares, yet hees no Cuccold.
But this Barnzy *knowes that his* Matilda
Skorning him with Haruy *playes the wanton;*

Knowes

Knowes it? nay desires it, and by prayers
Dayly begs of heau'n, that it for euer
May stand firme for him, yet hees no Cuccold:
And tis true, for Haruy *keeps* Matilda,
Fosters Barnzy, *and relieues his houshold,*
Buyes the Cradle, and begets the children,
Payes the Nurces eu'ry charge defraying,
And thus truly playes Matildas *husband:*
So that Barnzy *now becoms a cypher,*
And himselfe th'adultrer of Matilda.
Mock not him with hornes, the case is alterd,
Haruy *beares the wrong, he proues the Cuccold.*

The ninth *Epigramme.*

Buffe *loues fat vians, fat ale, fat all things,*
Keepes fat whores, fat offices, yet all men
Him fat only wish to feast the gallous.

The tenth *Epigramme.*

Smith *by sute diuorst, the knowne adultres*
Freshly weds againe; what ayles the mad-cap
By this fury? euen so theeues by frailty
Of their hempe reseru'd, againe the dismall
Tree embrace, againe the fatall halter.

The eleuenth *Epigramme.*

His late losse the Wiuelesse Higs *in order*
Eu'rywhere bewailes to friends, to strangers;
Tels them how by night a yongster armed
Saught his Wife (as hand in hand he held her)
With drawne sword to force, she cryed, he mainely
Roring ran for ayde, but (ah) returning
Fled was with the prize the beawty-forcer,
Whome in vaine he seekes, he threats, he followes.
Chang'd is Hellen, Hellen *hugs the stranger*
Safe as Paris *in the Greeke triumphing.*
Therewith his reports to teares he turneth,
Peirst through with the louely Dames remembrance;
Straight he sighes, he raues, his haire he teareth,
Forcing pitty still by fresh lamenting.
Cease vnworthy, worthy of thy fortunes,
Thou that couldst so faire a prize deliuer,
For feare vnregarded, vndefended,
Hadst no heart I thinke, I know no liuer.

The twelfth *Epigramme.*

Why droopst thou Trefeild? *will* Hurst *the Banker*
Make dice of thy bones? by heau'n he can not;

Can

Can not? whats the reason? ile declare it,
Th'ar all growne so pockie, and so rotten.

The seauenth Chapter, of the English Elegeick verse.

THe *Elegeick* verses challenge the next place, as being of all compound verses the simplest. They are deriu'd out of our owne naturall numbers as neere the imitation of the *Greekes* and *Latines*, as our heauy sillables will permit. The first verse is a meere licentiate *Iambick*; the second is fram'd of two vnited *Dimeters*. In the first *Dimeter* we are tyed to make the first foote either a *Trochy* or a *Spondee*, the second a *Trochy*, and the odde sillable of it alwaies long. The second *Dimeter* consists of two *Trochyes* (because it requires more swiftnes then the first) and an odde sillable, which being last, is euer common. I will giue you example both of *Elegye* and *Epigramme*, in this kinde.

An *Elegye*.

Constant to none, but euer false to me,
  Traiter still to loue through thy faint desires,

C

Not hope of pittie now nor vaine redresse
  Turns my griefs to teares, and renu'd laments
Too well thy empty vowes, and hollow thoughts
  Witnes both thy wrongs, and remorseles hart.
Rue not my sorrow, but blush at my name,
  Let thy bloudy cheeks guilty thoughts betray.
My flames did truly burne, thine made a shew,
  As fires painted are which no heate retayne,
Or as the glossy Pirop *faines to blaze,*
  But toucht cold appeares, and an earthy stone,
True cullours deck thy cheeks, false foiles thy brest,
  Frailer then thy light beawty is thy minde.
None canst thou long refuse, nor long affect,
  But turn'st feare with hopes, sorrow with delight,
Delaying, and deluding eu'ry way
  Those whose eyes are once with thy beawty chain'd.
Thrice happy man that entring first thy loue,
  Can so guide the straight raynes of his desires,
That both he can regard thee, and refraine:
  If grac't, firme he stands, if not, easely falls.

Example of *Epigrams*, in *Elegeick* verse.
The first *Epigramme.*

Arthure *brooks only those that brooke not him,*
  Those he most regards, and deuoutly serues:

                                        But

But them that grace him his great brau'ry skornes,
  Counting kindnesse all duty, not desert:
Arthure *wants forty pounds, tyres eu'ry friend,*
  But finds none that holds twenty due for him.

The second *Epigramme.*

If fancy can not erre which vertue guides,
  In thee Laura *then fancy can not erre.*

The third *Epigramme.*

Drue *feasts no Puritans, the churles he saith*
  Thanke no men, but eate, praise God, and depart.

The fourth *Epigramme.*

A wiseman wary liues, yet most secure,
  Sorrowes moue not him greatly, nor delights.
Fortune and death he skorning, only makes
  Th'earth his sober Inne, but still heau'n his home.

The fift *Epigramme.*

Thou telst me Barnzy Dawson *hath a wife,*
· *Thine he hath I graunt,* Dawson *hath a wife.*

C 2

The sixt *Epigramme*.

Drue *giues thee money, yet thou thankst not him,*
  But thankst God for him, like a godly man.
Suppose rude Puritan thou begst of him,
  And he saith God help, who's the godly man?

The seauenth *Epigramme*.

All wonders Barnzy *speakes, all grosely faind,*
  Speake some wonder once Barnzy, *speake the truth.*

The eight *Epigramme*.

None then should through thy beawty Lawra *pine,*
  Might sweet words alone ease a loue-sick heart:
But your sweet words alone that quit so well
  Hope of friendly deeds kill the loue-sick heart.

The ninth *Epigramme*.

At all thou frankly throwst, while Frank *thy wife*
Bars not Luke *the mayn,* Oteny *barre the bye.*
                                              The

The eight Chapter, of Ditties *and* Odes.

TO descend orderly from the more simple numbers to them that are more compounded, it is now time to handle such verses as are fit for *Ditties* or *Odes*; which we may call *Lyricall*, because they are apt to be soong to an instrument, if they were adorn'd with conuenient notes. Of that kind I will demonstrate three in this Chapter, and in the first we will proceede after the manner of the *Saphick* which is a *Trochaicall* verse as well as the *Hendicasillable* in Latine. The first three verses therefore in our English *Saphick* are meerely those *Trochaicks* which I handled in the sixt Chapter, excepting only that the first foote of either of them must euer of necessity be a *Spondee*, to make the number more graue. The fourth and last closing verse is compounded of three *Trochyes* together, to giue a more smooth farewell, as you may easily obserue in this Poeme made vpon a Triumph at *Whitehall*, whose glory was dasht with an vnwelcome showre, hindring the people from the desired sight of her Maiestie.

The English *Sapphick*.

Faiths pure shield the Christian Diana
Englands *glory crownd with all deuinenesse,*
Liue long with triumphs to blesse thy people
    At thy sight triumphing.
Loe they sound, the Knights in order armed
Entring threat the list, adrest to combat
For their courtly loues; he, hees the wonder
    Whome Eliza *graceth.*
Their plum'd pomp the vulgar heaps detaineth,
And rough steeds, let vs the still deuices
Close obserue, the speeches and the musicks
    Peacefull arms adorning.
But whence showres so fast this angry tempest,
Clowding dimme the place? behold Eliza
This day shines not here, this heard, the launces
    And thick heads do vanish.

The second kinde consists of *Dimeter*, whose
first foote may either be a *Sponde* or a *Trochy:* The
two verses following are both of them *Trochaical*,
and consist of foure feete, the first of either of
them being a *Spondee* or *Trochy*, the other three
                                                    only

only *Trochyes*. The fourth and last verse is made of two *Trochyes*. The number is voluble and fit to expresse any amorous conceit.

The Example.

Rose-cheekt Lawra *come*
Sing thou smoothly with thy beawties
Silent musick, either other
        Sweetely gracing.
Louely formes do flowe
From concent deuinely framed,
Heau'n is musick, and thy beawties
        Birth is heauenly.
These dull notes we sing
Discords neede for helps to grace them,
Only beawty purely louing
        Knowes no discord:
But still mooues delight
Like cleare springs renu'd by flowing,
Euer perfet, euer in them-
        selues eternall.

The third kind begins as the second kind ended, with a verse consisting of two *Trochy* feete,

C 4

and then as the second kind had in the middle two *Trochaick* verses of foure feete, so this hath three of the same nature, and ends in a *Dimeter* as the second began. The *Dimeter* may allow in the first place a *Trochy* or a *Spondee*, but no *Iambick*.

The Example.

Iust beguiler,
Kindest loue, yet only chastest,
Royall in thy smooth denyals,
Frowning or demurely smiling
            Still my pure delight.

Let me view thee
With thoughts and with eyes affected,
And if then the flames do murmur,
Quench them with thy vertue, charme them
            With thy stormy browes.

Heau'n so cheerefull
Laughs not euer, hory winter
Knowes his season, euen the freshest
Sommer mornes from angry thunder
            Iet not still secure.

                              The

The ninth Chapter, of the Anacreontick *verse.*

IF any shall demaund the reason why this number being in it selfe simple, is plac't after so many
compounded numbers, I answere, because I hold
it a number too licentiate for a higher place, and
in respect of the rest imperfect, yet is it passing
gracefull in our English toong, and will excellently fit the subiect of a *Madrigall*, or any other
lofty or tragicall matter. It consists of two feete,
the first may be either a *Sponde* or *Trochy*, the other
must euer represent the nature of a *Trochy*, as for
example:

> *Follow, followe*
> *Though with mischiefe*
> *Arm'd, like whirlewind*
> *Now she flyes thee;*
> *Time can conquer*
> *Loues vnkindnes;*
> *Loue can alter*
> *Times disgraces;*
> *Till death faint not*
> *Then but followe.*

G

Could I catch that
Nimble trayter
Skornefull Lawra,
Swift foote Lawra,
Soone then would I
Seeke auengement;
Whats th'auengement?
Euen submissely
Prostrate then to
Beg for mercye.

Thus haue I briefely described eight seuerall kinds of English numbers simple or compound. The first was our *Iambick* pure and licentiate. The second, that which I call our *Dimeter*, being deriued either from the end of our *Iambick*, or from the beginning of our *Trochaick*. The third which I deliuered was our English *Trochaick* verse. The fourth our English *Elegeick*. The fift, sixt, and seauenth, were our English *Sapphick*, and two other *Lyricall* numbers, the one beginning with that verse which I call our *Dimeter*, the other ending with the same. The eight and last was a kind of *Anacreontick* verse, handled in this Chapter. These numbers which by my long obseruation I haue found
agreeable

agreeable with the nature of our sillables, I haue
set forth for the benefit of our language, which I
presume the learned will not only imitate, but also
polish and amplifie with their owne inuentions.
Some eares accustomed altogether to the fatnes
of rime, may perhaps except against the cadences
of these numbers, but let any man iudicially examine them, and he shall finde they close of themselues so perfectly, that the help of rime were not
only in them superfluous, but also absurd. More-
ouer, that they agree with the nature of our English it is manifest, because they entertaine so willingly our owne British names, which the writers
in English Heroicks could neuer aspire vnto, and
euen our Rimers themselues haue rather delighted
in borrowed names then in their owne, though
much more apt and necessary. But it is now time
that I proceede to the censure of our sillables, and
that I set such lawes vpon them as by imitation,
reason, or experience, I can confirme. Yet before
I enter into that discourse, I will briefely recite,
and dispose in order all such feete as are necessary
for composition of the verses before described.
They are sixe in number, three whereof consist of
two sillables, and as many of three.

Feete of two sillables.

Iambick:				rĕuēnge.
Trochaick:	}	as	{	Bēawtĭe.
Sponde:				cōnstānt.

Feete of three sillables.

Tribrack:				mĭsĕrĭe.
Anapestick:	}	as	{	mĭsĕrīes.
Dactile:				Dēstĕnĭe.

*The tenth Chapter, of the quantity
of English sillables.*

THe *Greekes* in the quantity of their sillables were farre more licentious then the *Latines*, as *Martiall* in his Epigramme of *Earinon* witnesseth, saying, *Musas qui colimus seueriores*. But the English may very well challenge much more licence then either of them, by reason it stands chiefely vpon monasillables, which in expressing with the voyce, are of a heauy cariage, and for that cause the *Dactil*, *Trybrack*, and *Anapestick*
are

are not greatly mist in our verses. But aboue all
the accent of our words is diligently to be obseru'd, for chiefely by the accent in any language
the true value of the sillables is to be measured.
Neither can I remember any impediment except
position that can alter the accent of any sillable
in our English verse. For though we accent the
second of *Trumpington* short, yet is it naturally
long, and so of necessity must be held of euery
composer. Wherefore the first rule that is to be
obserued, is the nature of the accent, which we
must euer follow.

The next rule is position, which makes euery
sillable long, whether the position happens in one
or in two words, according to the manner of the
Latines, wherein is to be noted that *h* is no
letter.

Position is when a vowell comes before two
consonants, either in one or two words. In one, as
in *best*, *e* before *st*, makes the word *best* long by position. In two words, as in *setled loue*: *e* before *d* in
the last sillable of the first word, and *l* in the beginning of the second makes *led* in *setlēd* long by
position.

A vowell before a vowell is alwaies short, as,

flīīng, dīīng, gŏīng, vnlesse the accent alter it, as in *dĕnīīng.*

The dipthong in the midst of a word is al-waies long, as *plaīīng, deceīuing.*

The *Synalæphas* or *Elisions* in our toong are ei-ther necessary to auoid the hollownes and gaping in our verse as *to,* and *the, t'inchaunt, th'inchaunter,* or may be vsd at pleasure, as for *let vs,* to say *let's,* for *we will, wee'l,* for *euery, eu'ry,* for *they are, th'ar,* for *he is, hee's,* for *admired, admir'd,* and such like.

Also, because our English Orthography (as the French) differs from our common pronunciation, we must esteeme our sillables as we speake, not as we write, for the sound of them in a verse is to be valued, and not their letters, as for *follow,* we pronounce *follo,* for *perfect, perfet,* for *little, littel,* for *loue-sick, loue-sik,* for *honour, honor,* for *money, mony,* for *dangerous, dangerus,* for *raunsome, raun-sum,* for *though, tho,* and their like.

Deriuatiues hold the quantities of their pri-matiues, as *dĕuōut, dĕuōutelĭe, prŏphāne, prŏphānelĭe,* and so do the compositiues, as *dĕsēru'd ŭndĕseru'd.*

In words of two sillables, if the last haue a full and rising accent that sticks long vpon the voyce,
the

the first sillable is alwayes short, vnlesse position, or the dipthong doth make it long, as *dĕsīre*, *prĕ-sērue*, *dĕfīne*, *prŏphāne*, *rĕgārd*, *mănūre*, and such like.

If the like dissillables at the beginning haue double consonants of the same kind, we may vse the first sillable as common, but more naturally short, because in their pronunciation we touch but one of those double letters, as *ătēnd*, *ăpēare*, *ŏpōse*. The like we may say when silent and mel-ting consonants meete together, as *ădrēst*, *rĕdrēst*, *ŏprēst*, *rĕprēst*, *rĕtrīu'd*, and such like.

Words of two sillables that in their last sillable mayntayne a flat or falling accent, ought to hold their first sillable long, as *rīgŏr*, *glōrĭe*, *spīrĭt*, *fūrĭe*, *lābŏur*, and the like: *ăny*, *măny*, *prĕty*, *hŏly*, and their like, are excepted.

One obseruation which leades me to iudge of the difference of these dissillables whereof I last spake, I take from the originall monasillable, which if it be graue, as *shāde*, I hold that the first of *shādĭe* must be long, so *trūe*, *trūlĭe*, *hāue*, *hāuĭng*, *tūre*, *tūrĭng*.

Words of three sillables for the most part are deriued from words of two sillables, and from them take the quantity of their first sillable, as *flōrĭsh, flōrĭshīng* long, *hŏlĭe hŏlĭnes* short, but *mi*, in *mīser* being long, hinders not the first of *mĭsery* to be short, because the sound of the *i* is a little altred.

De, di, and *pro*, in trisillables (the second being short) are long, as *dēsŏlāte, dīlĭgēnt, prōdĭgall*.

Re is euer short, as *rĕmĕdĭe, rĕfĕrēnce, rĕdŏlēnt, rĕuĕrēnd*.

Likewise the first of these trisillables is short, as the first of *bĕnĕfit, gĕnĕrall, hĭdĕous, mĕmŏrĭe, nŭmĕrous, pĕnĕtrāte, sĕpĕrat, tĭmĕrous, vărĭānt, vărĭous*, and so may we esteeme of all that yeeld the like quicknes of sound.

In words of three sillables the quantity of the middle sillable is lightly taken from the last sillable of the originall dissillable, as the last of *dĕuīne*, ending in a graue or long accent, makes the second of *dĕuīnīng* also long, and so *ēspīe, ēspūīng, dĕnīe, dĕnūīng*: contrarywise it falles out if the last of the dissillable beares a flat or falling accent, as *glōrĭe, glōrĭīng, ēnuĭe, ēnuĭīng*, and so forth.

Words of more sillables are eyther borrowed and hold their owne nature, or are likewise deriu'd, and so follow the quantity of their primatiues,

tiues, or are knowne by their proper accents, or
may be easily censured by a iudiciall eare.

All words of two or more sillables ending with a
falling accent in *y* or *ye*, as *faĭrelĭe*, *dĕmurelĭe*, *beaw-
tĭe*, *pīttĭe*; or in *ue*, as *vērtuĕ*, *rēscuĕ*, or in *ow*, as
fŏllŏw, *hŏllŏw*, or in *e*, as *parlĕ*, *Daphnĕ*, or in *a*, as
Mannă, are naturally short in their last sillables:
neither let any man cauill at this licentiate abbre-
uiating of sillables, contrary to the custome of the
Latines, which made all their last sillables that ended in *u* long, but let him consider that our verse
of fiue feete, and for the most part but of ten sillables, must equall theirs of sixe feete and of many
sillables, and therefore may with sufficient reason
aduenture vpon this allowance. Besides, euery
man may obserue what an infinite number of
sillables both among the *Greekes* and *Romaines*
are held as common. But words of two sillables
ending with a rising accent in *y* or *ye*, as *denye*, *de-
scrye*, or in *ue*, as *ensue*, or in *ee*, as *foresee*, or in *oe*,
as *forgoe*, are long in their last sillables, vnlesse a
vowell begins the next word.

All monasillables that end in a graue accent
are euer long, as *wrāth*, *hāth*, *thēse*, *thōse*, *toōth*,
soōth, *thrōugh*, *dāy*, *plāy*, *feāte*, *speēde*, *strīfe*, *flōw*,
grōw, *shēw*.   D

The like rule is to be obserued in the last of dissillables, bearing a graue rising sound, as *deuine*, *delaie*, *retire*, *refuse*, *manure*, or a graue falling sound, as *fortune*, *pleasure*, *rampire*.

All such as haue a double consonant lengthning them, as *wārre*, *bārre*, *stārre*, *fūrre*, *mūrre*, appeare to me rather long then any way short.

There are of these kinds other, but of a lighter sound, that if the word following do begin with a vowell are short, as *doth*, *though*, *thou*, *now*, *they*, *two*, *too*, *flye*, *dye*, *true*, *due*, *see*, *are*, *far*, *you*, *thee*, and the like.

These monasillables are alwayes short, as *ă*, *thĕ*, *thĭ*, *shĕ*, *wĕ*, *bĕ*, *hĕ*, *nŏ*, *tŏ*, *gŏ*, *sŏ*, *dŏ*, and the like.

But if *i*, or *y*, are ioyn'd at the beginning of a word with any vowell, it is not then held as a vowell, but as a consonant, as *Ielosy*, *iewce*, *iade*, *ioy*, *Iudas*, *ye*, *yet*, *yel*, *youth*, *yoke*. The like is to be obseru'd in *w*, as *winde*, *wide*, *wood*: and in all words that begin with *va*, *ve*, *vi*, *vo*, or *vu*, as *vacant*, *vew*, *vine*, *voide*, and *vulture*.

All Monasillables or Polysillables that end in single consonants, either written, or sounded with single consonants, hauing a sharp liuely accent and

and standing without position of the word following, are short in their last sillable, as *scăb*, *flĕd*,
pārtĕd, *Gŏd*, *ŏf*, *ĭf*, *bāndŏg*, *ānguĭsh*, *sĭck*, *quĭck*,
rīuăl, *wĭll*, *pēoplĕ*, *sīmplĕ*, *comĕ*, *sŏme*, *hĭm*, *thĕm*,
frŏm, *sūmmŏn*, *thĕn*, *prŏp*, *prōspĕr*, *hōnoŭr*, *lāboŭr*,
thĭs, *hĭs*, *spēchĕs*, *gōddĕsse*, *pērfĕct*, *bŭt*, *whăt*, *thăt*,
and their like.

The last sillable of all words in the plurall number that haue two or more vowels before *s*, are
long, as *vertūes*, *duīes*, *miserīes*, *fellowēs*.

These rules concerning the quantity of our
English sillables I haue disposed as they came next
into my memory, others more methodicall, time
and practise may produce. In the meane season,
as the Grammarians leaue many sillables to the
authority of Poets, so do I likewise leaue many
to their iudgements; and withall thus conclude, that there is no Art begun
and perfected at one
enterprise.

FINIS.

ERRATA

The following emendations have been made in the text of the original :—

Page	Line		In the Original reads :
4	17	' tedious '	' tedions '
8	25	' do) '	' do,'
9		The page number is omitted	
10	18	*' the more the stroke '*	*' the more the more the stroke '*
28	3	*' But '*	*' Rut '*
41	25	*' dāy, plāy,'*	*' dāy plāy,'*

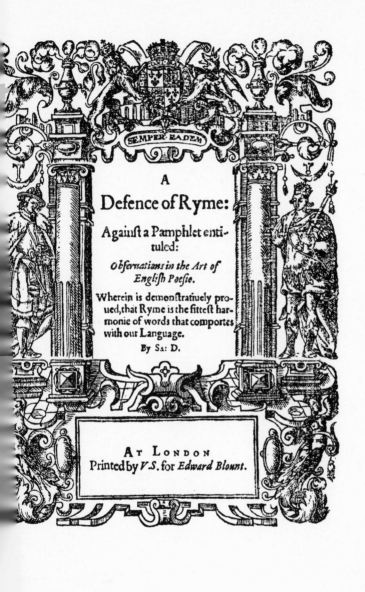

SEMPER EADEM

A

Defence of Ryme:

Against a Pamphlet enti-
tuled:

*Observations in the Art of
English Poesie.*

Wherein is demonstratiuely pro-
ued, that Ryme is the fittest harmonie of words that comportes
with our Language.

By Sa: D.

At London
Printed by *V. S.* for *Edward Blount.*

Note

THE ORIGINAL of this text is in the British Museum [fol. 644. k. 8 (2)], bound with *A Panegyrike Congratulatory* to King James the First. A list of the misprints which have been corrected in the text will be found on page 46.

G. B. H.

To all the Worthie Lo-

uers and learned Professors of Ryme,

within his Maiesties Dominions,

S. D.

Orthie Gentlemen, about a yeare since, vpon the great reproach giuen to the Professors of Rime, and the vse therof, I wrote a priuate letter, as a defence of mine owne vndertakings in that kinde, to a learned Gentleman a great friend of mine, then in Court. VVhich I did, rather to confirm my selfe in mine owne courses, and to hold him from being wonne from vs, then with any desire to publish the same to the world.

But now, seeing the times to promise a more regarde to the present condition of our writings, in respect of our Soueraignes happy inclination this way; whereby wee are rather to expect an incoragement to go on with what we do, then that any innouation should checke vs, with a shew of what / it would do in [G2 an other kinde, and yet doe nothing but depraue: I haue now giuen a greater body to the same Argument. And here present it to your view, vnder the patronage of a Noble Earle, who in bloud and nature is interessed to take our parte in this cause, with others, who cannot, I know, but holde deare the monuments that haue beene left vnto the world in this manner of composition. And who I trust will take in good parte this my defence, if not as it is my particular, yet in respect of the cause I vndertake, which I heere inuoke you all to protect.

Sa: D.

[G2*ᵛ*

TO
WILLIAM HERBERT EARLE
OF PEMBROOKE.

He Generall Custome, and vse of Ryme in this kingdome, Noble Lord, hauing beene so long (as if from a Graunt of Nature) held vnquestionable; made me to imagine that it lay altogither out of the way of contradiction, and was become so natural, as we should neuer haue had a thought to cast it off into reproch, or be made to thinke that it ill-became our language. But now I see, when there is opposition made to all things in the world by wordes, wee must nowe at length likewise fall to contend for words themselues; and make a question, whether they be right or not. For we are tolde how that our measures goe wrong, all Ryming is grosse, vulgare, barbarous, which if it be so, we haue lost much labour to no purpose: and for mine owne particular, I cannot but blame the fortune of the times and mine owne Genius that cast me vppon so wrong a course, drawne with the current of custome, and an vnexamined example. Hauing beene first incourag'd or fram'd thereunto by your most Worthy and Honourable Mother, receiuing the first notion for the formall ordering of those compositions at *Wilton*, which I must euer acknowledge to haue beene my best Schoole, and thereof alwayes am to hold a feeling and gratefull Memory.   Afterward, drawne farther on by the well-liking and approbation of my worthy Lord, the fosterer of mee and my *Muse*, I aduentured to bestow all my whole powers therein, perceiuing it agreed so well, both with the complexion of the times, and mine owne constitution, as I found not wherein I might better imploy me.   But yet now, vpon the great dis-couery of these new measures, threatning to ouer-throw the whole state of Ryme in this kingdom, I must either stand out to defend, or else be forced to forsake my selfe, and giue ouer all. And / though irresolution and a selfe distrust [G3 be the most apparent faults of my nature, and that the least checke of reprehension, if it fauour of reason, will as easily shake my resolution as any mans liuing: yet in this case I know not how I am growne more resolued, and before I sinke, willing to examine what those powers of iudgement are, that must beare me downe, and beat me off from the station of my profession, which by the law of nature I am set to defend.

And the rather for that this detractor (whose commendable Rymes albeit now himselfe an enemy to ryme, haue giuen heretofore to the world the best notice of his worth) is a man of faire parts, and good reputation, and therefore the reproach forcibly cast from such a hand may throw downe more at once then the labors of many shall in long time build vp againe, specially vpon the slippery foundation of opinion, and the worlds inconstancy, which knowes not well what it would haue, and:

Discit enim citius, meminitque libentius illud
Quod quis deridet quam quod probat & veneratur.

And he who is thus, become our vnkinde aduersarie, must pardon vs if we be as iealous of our fame and reputation, as hee is desirous of credite by his new-old arte, and must consider that we cannot, in a thing that concernes vs so neere, but haue a feeling of the wrong done, wherein euery Rymer in this vniuersall Iland as well as my selfe, stands interressed. So that if his charitie had equally drawne with his learning hee would haue

forborne to procure the enuie of so powerfull a
number vpon him, from whom he cannot but
expect the returne of a like measure of blame, and
onely haue made way to his owne grace, by the
proofe of his abilitie, without the disparaging of
vs, who would haue bin glad to haue stood quietly
by him, & perhaps commended his aduenture,
seeing that euermore of one science an other may
be borne, & that these Salies made out of the
quarter of our set knowledges, are the gallant
proffers onely of attemptiue spirits, and commendable though they worke no other effect than make
a Brauado: and I know it were *Indecens, & moro-
sum nimis, alienæ industriæ, modum ponere.* We
could well haue allowed of his numbers had he not
disgraced our Ryme; Which both Custome and
Nature doth most powerfully defend. Custome
that is before all Law, Nature that is aboue all
Arte. Euery language hath her proper number or
measure fitted to vse and delight, which, Custome
intertaining by the allowance of the Eare, doth /
indenize, and make naturall. All verse is but a [G3v
frame of wordes confinde within certaine measure;
differing from the ordinarie speach, and intro-
duced, the better to expresse mens conceipts, both
for delight and memorie. Which frame of wordes

consisting of *Rithmus* or *Metrum*, Number or Measure, are disposed into diuers fashions, according to the humour of the Composer and the set of the time; And these *Rhythmi* as *Aristotle* saith are familiar amongst all Nations, and *è naturali & sponte fusa compositione:* And they fall as naturally already in our language as euer Art can make them; being such as the Eare of it selfe doth marshall in their proper roomes, and they of themselues will not willingly be put out of their ranke; and that in such a verse as best comports with the Nature of our language. And for our Ryme (which is an excellencie added to this worke of measure, and a Harmonie, farre happier than any proportion Antiquitie could euer shew vs) dooth adde more grace, and hath more of delight than euer bare numbers, howsoeuer they can be forced to runne in our slow language, can possibly yeeld. Which, whether it be deriu'd of *Rhythmus*, or of *Romance* which were songs the *Bards* & *Druydes* about Rymes vsed, & therof were caled *Remensi*, as some Italians hold; or howsoeuer, it is likewise number and harmonie of words, consisting of an agreeing sound in the last silables of seuerall verses, giuing both to the Eare an Eccho of a delightfull report & to the Memorie a deeper

B

impression of what is deliuered therein. For as
Greeke and Latine verse consists of the number
and quantitie of sillables, so doth the English
verse of measure and accent. And though it doth
not strictly obserue long and short sillables, yet it
most religiously respects the accent: and as the
short and the long make number, so the Acute and
graue accent yeelde harmonie: And harmonie is
likewise number, so that the English verse then
hath number, measure and harmonie in the best
proportion of Musike. Which being more certain
& more resounding, works that effect of motion
with as happy successe as either the Greek or
Latin. And so naturall a melody is it, & so
vniuersall as it seems to be generally borne with
al the nations of the world, as an hereditary eloquence proper to all mankind. The vniuersallitie
argues the generall power of it: for if the Barbarian vse it, then it shews that it swais th'affection of the Barbarian, if ciuil nations practise it,
it proues that it works vpon the harts of ciuil
nations: If all, then that it hath a power in nature
on all. *Georgieuez de Turcarum moribus*, hath an
example of the Tur-/kish Rymes iust of the [G4
measure of our verse of eleuen sillables, in feminine Ryme: neuer begotten I am perswaded by

any example in *Europe*, but borne no doubt in *Scythia*, and brought ouer *Caucasus* and *Mount Taurus*. The Sclauonian and Arabian tongs acquaint a great part of *Asia* and *Affrique* with it, the Moscouite, Polack, Hungarian, German, Italian, French, and Spaniard vse no other harmonie of words. The Irish, Briton, Scot, Dane, Saxon, English, and all the Inhabiters of this Iland, either haue hither brought, or here found the same in vse. And such a force hath it in nature, or so made by nature, as the Latine numbers notwithstanding their excellencie, seemed not sufficient to satitsfie the eare of the world thereunto accustomed, without this Harmonicall cadence: which made the most learned of all nations labour with exceeding trauaile to bring those numbers likewise vnto it: which many did with that happinesse, as neither their puritie of tongue, nor their materiall contemplations are thereby any way disgraced, but rather deserue to be reuerenced of all gratefull posteritie, with the due regard of their worth. And for *Schola Salerna*, and those *Carmina Prouerbialia*, who finds not therein more precepts for vse, concerning diet, health, and conuersation, then *Cato*, *Theognes*, or all the Greekes and Latines can shew vs in that

kinde of teaching: and that in so few words, both
for delight to the eare, and the hold of memorie,
as they are to be imbraced of all modest readers
that studie to know and not to depraue.

Me thinkes it is a strange imperfection, that
men should thus ouer-runne the estimation of
good things with so violent a censure, as though
it must please none else, because it likes not them.
Whereas *Oportet arbitratores esse non contra-*
dictores eos qui verum iudicaturi sunt, saith *Arist.*
though he could not obserue it himselfe.　And
milde Charitie tells vs:

　　　　—— *non ego paucis*
　　Offendor maculis quas aut incuria fudit
　　Aut humana parum cauet natura. For all men
haue their errors, and we must take the best of
their powers, and leaue the rest as not appertaining vnto vs.

Ill customes are to be left, I graunt it: but I see
not howe that can be taken for an ill custome,
which nature hath thus ratified, all nations re-
ceiued, time so long confirmed, the effects such
as it performes those offices of motion for which
it is imployed; delighting the eare, stirring the
heart, and satisfying the iudge-/ment in such [G4*v*]
sort as I doubt whether euer single numbers will

do in our Climate, if they shew no more worke of
wonder then yet we see. And if euer they prooue
to become any thing, it must be by the approbation of many ages that must giue them their
strength for any operation, or before the world
will feele where the pulse, life, and enargie lies,
which now we are sure where to haue in our
Rymes, whose knowne frame hath those due staies
for the minde, those incounters of touch as makes
the motion certaine, though the varietie be infinite. Nor will the Generall sorte, for whom we
write (the wise being aboue bookes) taste these
laboured measures but as an orderly prose when
wee haue all done. For this kinde acquaintance
and continuall familiaritie euer had betwixt our
eare and this cadence, is growne to so intimate a
friendship, as it will nowe hardly euer be brought
to misse it. For be the verse neuer so good, neuer
so full, it seemes not to satisfie nor breede that
delight as when it is met and combined with a like
sounding accents. Which seemes as the iointure
without which it hangs loose, and cannot subsist,
but runnes wildely on, like a tedious fancie without a close: suffer then the world to inioy that
which it knowes, and what it likes. Seeing that
whatsoeuer force of words doth mooue, delight

and sway the affections of men, in what Scythian
sorte soeuer it be disposed or vttered: that is true
number, measure, eloquence, and the perfection
of speach: which I said, hath as many shapes as
there be tongues or nations in the world, nor can
with all the tyrannicall Rules of idle Rhetorique
be gouerned otherwise then custome, and present
obseruation will allow. And being now the trym,
and fashion of the times, to sute a man otherwise
cannot but giue a touch of singularity, for when
hee hath all done, hee hath but found other
clothes to the same body, and peraduenture not so
fitting as the former. But could our Aduersary
hereby set vp the musicke of our times to a higher
note of iudgement and discretion, or could these
new lawes of words better our imperfections, it
were a happy attempt; but when hereby we shall
but as it were change prison, and put off these
fetters to receiue others, what haue we gained, as
good still to vse ryme and a little reason, as neither
ryme nor reason, for no doubt as idle wits will
write, in that kinde, as do now in this, imitation
wil after, though it breake her necke. *Scribimus
indocti doctique poemata passim.* And this multitude
of idle writers can be no disgrace to the good, for
the same fortune in one proportion or other is

proper in a like season / to all States in their [G5 turne: and the same vnmeasureable confluence of Scriblers hapned, when measures were most in vse among the Romanes, as we finde by this reprehension,

Mutauit mentem populus leuis, & calet vno
Scribendi studio, pueri, patrésque seueri,
Fronde comas vincti cœnant, & carmina dictant.

So that their plentie seemes to haue bred the same waste and contempt as ours doth now, though it had not power to disvalew what was worthy of posteritie, nor keep backe the reputation of excellencies, destined to continue for many ages. For seeing it is matter that satisfies the iudiciall, appeare it in what habite it will, all these pretended proportions of words, howsoeuer placed, can be but words, and peraduenture serue but to embroyle our vnderstanding, whilst seeking to please our eare, we inthrall our iudgement: to delight an exterior sense, wee smoothe vp a weake confused sense, affecting sound to be vnsound, and all to seeme *Seruum pecus*, onely to imitate the Greekes and Latines, whose felicitie, in this kind, might be something to themselues, to whome their owne *idioma* was naturall, but to vs it can yeeld no other commoditie then a sound. We admire them

not for their smooth-gliding words, nor their
measures, but for their inuentions: which treasure,
if it were to be found in Welch, and Irish, we
should hold those languages in the same estimation, and they may thanke their sword that made
their tongues so famous and vniuersall as they are.
For to say truth, their Verse is many times but a
confused deliuerer of their excellent conceits,
whose scattered limbs we are faine to looke out
and ioyne together, to discerne the image of what
they represent vnto vs. And euen the Latines,
who professe not to be so licentious as the Greekes,
shew vs many times examples but of strange
crueltie, in torturing and dismembring of wordes
in the middest, or disioyning such as naturally
should be married and march together, by setting
them as farre asunder, as they can possibly stand:
that sometimes, vnlesse the kind reader, out of his
owne good nature, wil stay them vp by their
measure, they will fall downe into flatte prose, and
sometimes are no other indeede in their naturall
sound: and then againe, when you finde them
disobedient to their owne Lawes, you must hold
it to be *licentia poetica*, and so dispensable. The
striuing to shew their changable measures in the
varietie of their Odes, haue beene very painefull

no doubt vnto them, and forced them thus to disturbe the quiet streame of their wordes, / [G5ᵛ which by a naturall succession otherwise desire to follow in their due course.

But such affliction doth laboursome curiositie still lay vpon our best delights (which euer must be made strange and variable) as if Art were ordained to afflict Nature, and that we could not goe but in fetters. Euery science, euery profession, must be so wrapt vp in vnnecessary intrications, as if it were not to fashion, but to confound the vnderstanding, which makes me much to distrust man, and feare that our presumption goes beyond our abilitie, and our Curiositie is more than our Iudgement: laboring euer to seeme to be more than we are, or laying greater burthens vpon our mindes, then they are well able to beare, because we would not appeare like other men.

And indeed I haue wished there were not that multiplicitie of Rymes as is vsed by many in Sonets, which yet we see in some so happily to succeed, and hath beene so farre from hindering their inuentions, as it hath begot conceit beyond expectation, and comparable to the best inuentions of the world: for sure in an eminent spirit whome Nature hath fitted for that mysterie, Ryme is no impediment to his conceit, but rather giues him wings to mount and carries him, not out of his course, but as it were beyond his power to a farre happier flight. Al excellencies being sold vs at the hard price of labour, it followes, where we bestow most thereof, we buy the best successe: and Ryme being farre more laborious then loose measures (whatsoeuer is obiected) must needs, meeting with wit and industry, breed greater and worthier effects in our language. So that if our labours haue wrought out a manumission from bondage, and that wee goe at libertie, notwithstanding these ties, wee are no longer the slaues of Ryme, but we make it a most excellent instrument to serue vs. Nor is this certaine limit obserued in Sonnets, any tyrannicall bounding of the conceit, but rather a reducing it in *girum*, and a iust forme, neither too long for the shortest proiect, nor too short for the longest, being but onely imployed for a present passion. For the body of our imagination, being as an vnformed *Chaos* without fashion, without day, if by the diuine power of the spirit it be wrought into an Orbe of order and forme, is it not more pleasing to Nature, that desires a certaintie, and comports not with that which is infinite, to haue these clozes, rather than, not to know where to

end, or how farre to goe, especially seeing our
passions are often without measure: and wee finde
the best / of the latines many times, either not [G6
concluding, or els otherwise in the end then they
began. Besides, is it not most delightfull to see
much excellently ordred in a small-roome, or little,
gallantly disposed and made to fill vp a space of
like capacitie, in such sort, that the one would not
appeare so beautifull in a larger circuite, nor the
other do well in a lesse: which often we find to be
so, according to the powers of nature, in the
workeman. And these limited proportions, and
rests of Stanzes: consisting of 6. 7. or 8. lines are
of that happines, both for the disposition of the
matter, the apt planting the sentence where it may
best stand to hit, the certaine close of delight with
the full body of a iust period well carried, is such,
as neither the Greekes or Latines euer attained
vnto. For their boundlesse running on, often so
confounds the Reader, that hauing once lost himselfe, must either giue off vnsatisfied, or vn-
certainely cast backe to retriue the escaped sence,
and to find way againe into his matter.

Me thinkes we should not so soone yeeld our
consents captiue to the authoritie of Antiquitie,
vnlesse we saw more reason: all our vnderstandings

are not to be built by the square of *Greece* and
Italie. We are the children of nature as well as
they, we are not so placed out of the way of iudgement, but that the same Sunne of Discretion
shineth vppon vs, wee haue our portion of the
same vertues as well as of the same vices, *Et
Catilinam Quocunque in populo videas, quocunque
sub axe.* Time and the turne of things bring about
these faculties according to the present estimation:
and, *Res temporibus non tempora rebus seruire oppor-
tet.* So that we must neuer rebell against vse:
Quem penes arbitrium est, & vis & norma loquendi.
It is not the obseruing of *Trochaicques* nor their
Iambicques, that wil make our writings ought the
wiser: All their Poesie, all their Philosophie is
nothing, vnlesse we bring the discerning light of
conceipt with vs to apply it to vse. It is not bookes,
but onely that great booke of the world, and the
all-ouerspreading grace of heauen that makes men
truely iudiciall. Nor can it be but a touch of
arrogant ignorance, to hold this or that nation
Barbarous, these or those times grosse, considering
how this manifold creature man, wheresoeuer hee
stand in the world, hath alwayes some disposition
of worth, intertaines the order of societie, affects
that which is most in vse, and is eminent in some

one thing or other, that fits his humour and the times. The Grecians held all other nations barbarous but themselues, yet *Pirrhus* when he saw the well ordered marching of the Ro- / [G6*v* manes, which made them see their presumptuous errour, could say it was no barbarous maner of proceeding. The *Gothes*, *Vandales* and *Longobards*, whose comming downe like an inundation ouerwhelmed, as they say, al the glory of learning in *Europe*, haue yet left vs still their lawes and custanes, as the originalls of most of the prouinciall constitutions of Christendome; which well considered with their other courses of gouernement, may serue to cleere them from this imputation of ignorance. And though the vanquished neuer yet spake well of the Conquerour: yet euen thorow the vnsound couerings of malediction appeare those monuments of trueth, as argue wel their worth and proues them not without iudgement, though without Greeke and Latine.

Will not experience confute vs, if wee shoulde say the state of *China*, which neuer heard of Anapestiques, Trochies, and Tribracques, were grosse, barbarous, and vnciuile? And is it not a most apparant ignorance, both of the succession of learning in *Europe*, and the generall course of things, *to say, that all lay pittifully deformed in those lacke-lèarning times from the declining of the Romane Empire, till the light of the Latine tongue was reuiued by* Rewcline, Erasmus *and* Moore. When for three hundred yeeres before them about the comming downe of *Tamburlaine* into *Europe, Franciscus Petrarcha* (who then no doubt likewise found whom to imitate) shewed all the best notions of learning, in that degree of excellencie, both in Latin, Prose and Verse, and in the vulgare Italian, as all the wittes of posteritie haue not yet much ouer-matched him in all kindes to this day: his great Volumes written in Moral Philosophie, shew his infinite reading, and most happy power of disposition: his twelue Æglogues, his *Affrica* containing nine Bookes of the last Punicke warre, with his three Bookes of Epistles in Latine verse, shew all the transformations of wit and inuention, that a Spirite naturally borne to the inheritance of Poetrie & iudiciall knowledge could expresse: All which notwithstanding wrought him not that glory & fame with his owne Nation, as did his Poems in Italian, which they esteeme aboue al whatsoeuer wit could haue inuented in any other forme then wherein it is: which questionles they wil not change with the best measures, Greeks or Latins can shew

them; howsoeuer our Aduersary imagines. Nor
could this very same innouation in Verse, begun
amongst them by *C. Tolomæi*, but die in the
attempt, and was buried as soone as it came borne,
neglected as a prodigious & vnnaturall issue
amongst them: nor could / it neuer induce [H1
Tasso the wonder of *Italy*, to write that admirable
Poem of *Ierusalem*, comparable to the best of the
ancients, in any other forme then the accustomed
verse. And with *Petrarch* liued his scholer *Boc-
cacius*, and neere about the same time, *Iohannis
Rauenensis*, and from these *tanquam ex equo
Troiano*, seemes to haue issued all those famous
Italian Writers, *Leonardus Aretinus*, *Laurentius
Valla*, *Poggius*, *Blondus*, and many others. Then
Emanuel Chrysolaras a Constantinopolitan gentle-
man, renowmed for his learning and vertue, being
imployed by *Iohn Paleologus* Emperour of the
East, to implore the ayde of christian Princes, for
the succouring of perishing *Greece:* and vnderstanding in the meane time, how *Baiazeth* was
taken prisoner by *Tamburlan*, and his country
freed from danger, stayed still at *Venice*, and there
taught the Greeke tongue, discontinued before, in
these parts the space of seauen hundred yeeres.
Him followed *Bessarion*, *George Trapezantius*,

Theodore Gaza, & others, transporting Philosophie beaten by the Turke out of *Greece* into
christendome.   Hereupon came that mightie
confluence of Learning in these parts, which
returning, as it were *per postliminium*, and heere
meeting then with the new inuented stampe of
Printing, spread it selfe indeed in a more vniuersall sorte then the world euer heeretofore had it.
When *Pomponius Lætus, AEneas Syluius, Angelus
Politianus, Hermolaus Barbarus, Iohannes Picus de
Mirandula* the miracle & Phœnix of the world,
adorned *Italie*, and wakened vp other Nations
likewise with this desire of glory, long before it
brought foorth, *Rewclen, Erasmus*, and *Moore*,
worthy men I confesse, and the last a great orna-
ment to this land, and a Rymer.   And yet long
before all these, and likewise with these, was not
our Nation behind in her portion of spirite and
worthinesse, but concurrent with the best of all
this lettered worlde: witnesse venerable *Bede*, that
flourished aboue a thousand yeeres since: *Aldel-
mus Durotelmus* that liued in the yeere 739. of
whom we finde this commendation registred.
*Omnium Poetarum sui temporis facilè primus, tantæ
eloquentiæ, maiestatis & eruditionis homo fuit, vt
nunquam satis admirari possim vnde illi in tam*

barbara ac rudi ætate facundia accreuerit, vsque adeo
omnibus numeris tersa, elegans & rotunda, versus
edidit cum antiquitate de palma contendentes. Witnesse *Iosephus Deuonius,* who wrote *de bello*
Troiano, in so excellent manner, and so neere
resembling Antiquitie, as Printing his Worke
beyond the Seas, they haue ascribed it to *Cornelius*
Nepos, one of the Ancients.

What should I name *Walterus Mape, Gulielmus*
Nigellus, | *Geruasius Tilburiensis, Bracton,* [Hiv
Bacon, Ockam, and an infinite Catalogue of
excellent men, most of them liuing about foure
hundred yeares since, and haue left behinde them
monuments of most profound iudgement and
learning in all sciences. So that it is but the clowds
gathered about our owne iudgement that makes vs
thinke all other ages wrapt vp in mists, and the
great distance betwixt vs, that causes vs to imagine
men so farre off, to be so little in respect of our
selues. We must not looke vpon the immense
course of times past, as men ouer-looke spacious
and wide countries, from off high Mountaines and
are neuer the neere to iudge of the true Nature of
the soyle, or the particular syte and face of those
territories they see. Nor must we thinke, viewing
the superficiall figure of a region in a Mappe that

c

wee know strait the fashion and place as it is. Or
reading an Historie (which is but a Mappe of
men, and dooth no otherwise acquaint vs with the
true Substance of Circumstances, than a superficiall Card dooth the Sea-man with a Coast neuer
seene, which alwayes prooues other to the eye than
the imagination forecast it) that presently wee
know all the world, and can distinctly iudge of
times, men and maners, iust as they were. When
the best measure of man is to be taken by his owne
foote, bearing euer the neerest proportion to
himselfe, and is neuer so farre different and
vnequall in his powers, that he hath all in perfection at one time, and nothing at an other. The
distribution of giftes are vniuersall, and all seasons
hath them in some sort. We must not thinke, but
that there were *Scipioes*, *Cæsars*, *Catoes* and *Pom-
peies*, borne elsewhere then at *Rome*, the rest of the
world hath euer had them in the same degree of
nature, though not of state. And it is our weakenesse that makes vs mistake, or misconceiue in
these deliniations of men the true figure of their
worth. And our passion and beliefe is so apt to
leade vs beyond truth, that vnlesse we try them by
the iust compasse of humanitie, and as they were
men, we shall cast their figures in the ayre when

we should make their models vpon Earth. It is
not the contexture of words, but the effects of
Action that giues glory to the times: we finde they
had *mercurium in pectore* though not *in lingua*, and
in all ages, though they were not Ciceronians, they
knew the Art of men, which onely is, *Ars Artium*,
the great gift of heauen, and the chiefe grace and
glory on earth, they had the learning of Gouernement, and ordring their State, Eloquence inough
to shew their iudgements. And it seemes / the [H2
best times followed *Lycurgus* councell: *Literas ad
vsum saltem discebant, reliqua omnis disciplina erat,
vt pulchre parerent vt labores perferrent &c.* Had
not vnlearned *Rome* laide the better foundation,
and built the stronger frame of an admirable state,
eloquent *Rome* had confounded it vtterly, which
we saw, ranne the way of all confusion, the plaine
course of dissolution in her greatest skill: and
though she had not power to vndoe her selfe, yet
wrought she so that she cast her selfe quite away
from the glory of a common-wealth, and fell vpon
that forme of state she euer most feared and
abhorred of all other: and then scarse was there
seene any shadowe of pollicie vnder her first
Emperours, but the most horrible and grosse confusion that could bee conceued, notwithstanding

it stil indured, preseruing not only a Monarchie, locked vp in her own limits, but therewithall held vnder her obedience, so many Nations so farre distant, so ill affected, so disorderly commanded & vniustly conquerd, as it is not to be attributed to any other fate but to the first frame of that common-wealth, which was so strongly ioynted and with such infinite combinations interlinckt, as one naile or other euer held vp the Maiestie thereof. There is but one learning, which *omnes gentes habent scriptum in cordibus suis*, one and the selfe-same spirit that worketh in all. We haue but one body of Iustice, one body of Wisedome throughout the whole world, which is but apparaled according to the fashion of euery nation.

Eloquence and gay wordes are not of the Substance of wit, it is but the garnish of a nice time, the Ornaments that doe but decke the house of a State, *& imitatur publicos mores:* Hunger is as well satisfied with meat serued in pewter as siluer. Discretion is the best measure, the rightest foote in what habit soeuer it runne. *Erasmus*, *Rewcline* and *More*, brought no more wisdome into the world with all their new reuiued wordes then we finde was before, it bred not a profounder Diuine than Saint *Thomas*, a greater Lawyer than *Bartolus*, a more accute Logician than *Scotus:* nor are the effects of all this great amasse of eloquence so admirable or of that consequence, but that *impexa illa antiquitas* can yet compare with them. Let vs go no further, but looke vpon the wonderfull Architecture of this state of *England*, and see whether they were deformed times, that could giue it such a forme. Where there is no one the least piller of Maiestie, but was set with most profound iudgement and borne vp with the iust conueniencie of Prince and people. No Court of Iustice, / but laide by the Rule and Square of Nature, [H2v and the best of the best commonwealths that euer were in the world. So strong and substantial, as it hath stood against al the storms of factions, both of beliefe & ambition, which so powerfully beat vpon it, and all the tempestuous alterations of humorous times whatsoeuer. Being continually in all ages furnisht with spirites fitte to maintaine the maiestie of her owne greatnes, and to match in an equall concurrencie all other kingdomes round about her with whome it had to incounter. But this innouation, like a Viper, must euer make way into the worlds opinion, thorow the bowelles of her owne breeding, & is alwayes borne with reproch

in her mouth; the disgracing others is the best
grace it can put on, to winne reputation of wit, and
yet is it neucr so wise as it would seeme, nor doth
the world euer get so much by it, as it imagineth:
which being so often deceiued, and seeing it neuer
performes so much as it promises, me thinkes men
should neuer giue more credite vnto it. For, let vs
change neuer so often, wee can not change man,
our imperfections must still runne on with vs. And
therefore the wiser Nations haue taught menne
alwayes to vse, *Moribus legibusque presentibus etiamsi
deteriores sint.* The Lacedemonians, when a Musi-
tian, thincking to winne him-selfe credite by his
new inuention, and be before his fellowes, had
added one string more to his Crowde, brake his
fiddle, and banished him the Cittie, holding the
Innouator, though in the least things, dangerous
to a publike societie. It is but a fantastike giddi-
nesse to forsake the way of other men, especially
where it lies tollerable: *Vbi nunc est respublica, ibi
simus potius quam dum illam veterem sequimur,
simus in nulla.* But shal we not tend to perfection?
Yes, and that euer best by going on in the course
we are in, where we haue aduantage, being so farre
onward, of him that is but now setting forth. For
we shall neuer proceede, if wee be euer beginning,

nor arriue at any certayne Porte, sayling with all windes that blow: *Non conualescit planta quæ sæpius transfertur*, and therefore let vs hold on in the course wee haue vndertaken, and not still be wandring. Perfection is not the portion of man, and if it were, why may wee not as well get to it this way as an other? and suspect these great vndertakers, lest they haue conspired with enuy to betray our proceedings, and put vs by the honor of our attempts, with casting vs backe vpon an other course, of purpose to ouerthrow the whole action of glory when we lay the fairest for it, and were so neere our hopes? I thanke God that / I am none of these great Schollers, if thus their [H3 hie knowledges doe but giue them more eyes to looke out into vncertaintie and confusion, accounting my selfe, rather beholding to my ignorance, that hath set me in so lowe an vnder-roome of conceipt with other men, and hath giuen me as much distrust, as it hath done hope, daring not aduenture to goe alone, but plodding on the plaine tract I finde beaten by Custome and the Time, contenting me with what I see in vse. And surely mee thinkes these great wittes should rather seeke to adorne, than to disgrace the present, bring something to it, without taking from it what it hath. But it is euer the misfortune of Learning, to be wounded by her owne hand. *Stimulos dat emula virtus*, and when there is not abilitie to match what is, malice wil finde out ingines, either to disgrace or ruine it, with a peruerse incounter of some new impression: and which is the greatest misery, it must euer proceed from the powers of the best reputation, as if the greatest spirites were ordained to indanger the worlde, as the grosse are to dishonour it, and that we were to expect *ab optimis periculum, à pessimis dedecus publicum.* Emulation the strongest pulse that beates in high mindes, is oftentimes a winde, but of the worst effect: For whilst the Soule comes disappoynted of the obiect it wrought on, it presently forges an other, and euen cozins it selfe, and crosses all the world, rather than it wil stay to be vnder hir desires, falling out with all it hath, to flatter and make faire that which it would haue. So that it is the ill successe of our longings that with *Xerxes* makes vs to whippe the Sea, and send a cartel of defiance to mount *Athos:* and the fault laide vpon others weakenesse, is but a presumptuous opinion of our owne strength, who must not seeme to be maistered. But had our Aduersary taught vs by his owne proceedings, this way of perfection, and

therein fram'd vs a Poeme of that excellencie as
should haue put downe all, and beene the maister-
peece of these times, we should all haue admired
him. But to depraue the present forme of writing,
and to bring vs nothing but a few loose and vn-
charitable Epigrammes, and yet would make vs
belieue those numbers were come to raise the
glory of our language, giueth vs cause to suspect
the performance, and to examine whether this
new Arte, *constat sibi*, or, *aliquid sit dictum quod
non sit dictum prius*.

First we must heere imitate the Greekes and
Latines, and yet we are heere shewed to disobey
them, euen in their owne numbers and quantities:
taught to produce what they make short, and /
make short what they produce: made beleeue [H3ᵛ
to be shewd measures in that forme we haue not
seene, and no such matter: tolde that heere is the
perfect Art of versifying, which in conclusion is
yet confessed to be vnperfect, as if our Aduersary
to be opposite to vs, were become vnfaithfull to
himselfe, and seeking to leade vs out of the way of
reputation, hath aduentured to intricate and confound him in his owne courses, running vpon most
vn-euen groundes, with imperfect rules, weake
proofes, and vnlawfull lawes. Whereunto the

world, I am perswaded, is not so vnreasonable as
to subscribe, considering the vniust authoritie of
the Law-giuer. For who hath constituted him to
be the *Radamanthus* thus to torture sillables, and
adiudge them their perpetuall doome, setting his
Theta or marke of condemnation vppon them, to
indure the appoynted sentence of his crueltie, as
hee shall dispose. As though there were that
disobedience in our wordes, as they would not be
ruled or stand in order without so many intricate
Lawes, which would argue a great peruersenesse
amongst them, according to that, *in pessima re-
publica plurimæ leges*: or, that they were so farre
gone from the quiet freedome of nature, that they
must thus be brought backe againe by force. And
now in what case were this poore state of words,
if in like sorte another tyrant the next yeere should
arise and abrogate these lawes and ordaine others
cleane contrary according to his humor, and say
that they were onely right, the others vniust, what
disturbance were there here, to whome should we
obey? Were it not farre better to holde vs fast to
our old custome, than to stand thus distracted with
vncertaine Lawes, wherein Right shal haue as
many faces as it pleases Passion to make it, that
wheresoeuer mens affections stand, it shall still

looke that way. What trifles doth our vnconstant
curiositie cal vp to contend for, what colours are
there laid vpon indifferent things to make them
seeme other then they are, as if it were but only
to intertaine contestation amongst men; who
standing according to the prospectiue of their
owne humour, seeme to see the selfe same things
to appeare otherwise to them, than either they doe
to other, or are indeede in themselues, being but
all one in nature. For what a doe haue we heere,
what strange precepts of Arte about the framing
of an Iambique verse in our language, which when
all is done, reaches not by a foote, but falleth out
to be the plaine ancient verse consisting of tenne
sillables or fiue feete, which hath euer beene vsed
amongest vs time out of minde. And for all this /
cunning and counterfeit name can or will be [H4
any other in nature then it hath beene euer heretofore: and this new *Dimeter* is but the halfe of this
verse diuided in two, and no other then the *Cæsura*
or breathing place in the middest thereof, and
therefore it had bene as good to haue put two lines
in one, but only to make them seeme diuerse. Nay
it had beene much better for the true English
reading and pronouncing thereof, without violat-
ing the accent, which now our Aduersarie hath

heerein most vnkindely doone: for, being, as wee
are to sound it, according to our English March,
we must make a rest, and raise the last sillable,
which falles out very vnnaturall in *Desolate*,
Funerall, *Elizabeth*, *Prodigall*, and in all the rest
sauing the Monosillables.   Then followes the
English *Trochaicke*, which is saide to bee a simple
verse, and so indeede it is, being without Ryme;
hauing here no other grace then that in sound it
runnes like the knowne measure of our former
ancient Verse, ending (as we terme it according to
the French) in a feminine foote, sauing that it is
shorter by one sillable at the beginning, which is
not much missed, by reason it falles full at the last.
Next comes the *Elegiacke*, being the fourth kinde,
and that likewise is no other then our old accustomed measure of fiue feete; if there be any
difference, it must be made in the reading, and
therein wee must stand bound to stay where often
we would not, and sometimes either breake the
accent, or the due course of the word.   And now
for the other foure kinds of numbers, which are to
be employed for *Odes*, they are either of the same
measure, or such as haue euer beene familiarly
vsed amongst vs. So that of all these eight seuerall
kindes of new promised numbers you see what we

haue. Onely what was our owne before, and the
same but apparelled in forraine Titles, which had
they come in their kinde and naturall attire of
Ryme, wee should neuer haue suspected that they
had affected to be other, or sought to degenerate
into strange manners, which now we see was the
cause why they were turnd out of their proper
habite, and brought in as Aliens, onely to induce
men to admire them as farre-commers. But see the
power of Nature, it is not all the artificiall couerings of wit that can hide their natiue and originall
condition which breakes out thorow the strongest
bandes of affectation, and will be it selfe, doe
Singularitie what it can. And as for those ima-
gined quantities of sillables, which haue bin euer
held free and indifferent in our language, who can
inforce vs to take knowledge of them, being *in
nullius verba iurati*, & ow-/ing fealty to no [H4v
forraine inuention; especially in such a case where
there is no necessitie in Nature, or that it imports
either the matter or forme, whether it be so, or
otherwise. But euery Versifier that wel obserues
his worke, findes in our language, without all these
vnnecessary precepts, what numbers best fitte the
Nature of her Idiome, and the proper places
destined to such accents, as she will not let in, to

any other roomes then into those for which they were borne. As for example, you cannot make this fall into the right sound of a Verse.

None thinkes reward rendred worthy his worth:
vnlesse you thus misplace the accent vppon *Rendrèd* and *Worthìe*, contrary to the nature of these wordes: which sheweth that two feminine numbers (or Trochies, if so you wil call them) will not succeede in the third and fourth place of the Verse. And so likewise in this case,

Though Death doth consume, yet Virtue preserues.
it will not be a Verse, though it hath the iust sillables, without the same number in the second, and the altering of the fourth place, in this sorte:

Though Death doth ruine, Virtue yet preserues.

Againe, who knowes not that we cannot kindely answere a feminine number with a masculine Ryme, or (if you will so terme it) a *Trochei* with a *Sponde*, as *Weakenes* with *Confesse, Nature* and *Indure*, onely for that thereby wee shall wrong the accent, the chiefe Lord and graue Gouernour of Numbers. Also you cannot in a Verse of foure feete, place a *Trochei* in the first, without the like offence, as,   *Yearely out of his watry Cell.*
for so you shall sound it *Yeareliè* which is vnnaturall. And other such like obseruations vsually

occurre, which Nature and a iudiciall eare, of
themselues teach vs readily to auoyde.

But now for whom hath our Aduersary taken
all this paines? For the Learned, or for the
Ignorant, or for himselfe, to shew his owne skill?
If for the Learned, it was to no purpose, for euerie
Grammarian in this land hath learned his *Prosodia*,
and alreadie knowes all this Arte of Numbers: if
for the Ignorant, it was vaine: For if they become
Versifiers, wee are like to haue leane Numbers,
instede of fat Ryme: and if *Tully* would haue his
Orator skilld in all the knowledges appertaining
to God and man, what should they haue, who
would be a degree aboue Orators? Why then it
was to shew his owne skill, and what himselfe had
obserued: so he might well haue done, without
doing wrong to / the fame of the liuing, and [H5
wrong to *England*, in seeking to lay reproach
vppon her natiue ornaments, and to turne the faire
streame and full course of her accents, into the
shallow current of a lesse vncertaintie, cleane out
of the way of her knowne delight. And I had
thought it could neuer haue proceeded from the
pen of a Scholler (who sees no profession free from
the impure mouth of the scorner) to say the
reproach of others idle tongues is the curse of

Nature vpon vs, when it is rather her curse vpon him, that knowes not how to vse his tongue. What, doth he think himselfe is now gotten so farre out of the way of contempt, that his numbers are gone beyond the reach of obloquie, and that how friuolous, or idle soeuer they shall runne, they shall be protected from disgrace, as though that light rymes and light numbers did not weigh all alike in the graue opinion of the wise. And that it is not Ryme, but our ydle Arguments that hath brought downe to so base a reckning, the price and estimation of writing in this kinde. When the few good things of this age, by comming together in one throng and presse with the many bad, are not discerned from them, but ouer-looked with them, and all taken to be alike. But when after-times shall make a quest of inquirie, to examine the best of this Age, peraduenture there will be found in the now contemned recordes of Ryme, matter not vnfitting the grauest Diuine, and seuerest Lawyer in this kingdome. But these things must haue the date of Antiquitie, to make them reuerend and

Simplicius authentical: For euer in the collation of Writers,
longè posita men rather weigh their age then their merite, &
miramur. *legunt priscos cum reuerentia, quando coetaneos non possunt sine inuidia.* And let no writer in Ryme be

any way discouraged in his endeuour by this braue allarum, but rather animated to bring vp all the best of their powers, and charge withall the strength of nature and industrie vpon contempt, that the shew of their reall forces may turne backe insolencie into her owne holde. For, be sure that innouation neuer workes any ouerthrow, but vpon the aduantage of a carelesse idlenesse. And let this make vs looke the better to our feete, the better to our matter, better to our maners. Let the Aduersary that thought to hurt vs, bring more profit and honor, by being against vs, then if he had stoode still on our side. For that (next to the awe of heauen) the best reine, the strongst hand to make men keepe their way, is that which their enemy beares vpon them: and let this be the benefite wee make by being oppugned, and the meanes to redeeme backe the good opinion, / [H5v vanitie and idlenesse haue suffered to be wonne from vs; which, nothing but substance and matter can effect. for,

   Scribendi rectè sapere est & principium & fons.

When we heare Musicke, we must be in our eare, in the vtter-roome of sense, but when we intertaine iudgement, we retire into the cabinet and innermost withdrawing chamber of the soule:

D

And it is but as Musicke for the eare,
>   *Verba sequi fidibus modulanda Latinis.*
but it is a worke of power for the soule.
>   *Numerósque modósque ediscere vitæ.*

The most iudiciall and worthy spirites of this
Land are not so delicate, or will owe so much to
their eare, as to rest vppon the out-side of wordes,
and be intertained with sound: seeing that both
Number, Measure, and Ryme, is but as the
ground or seate, whereupon is raised the work that
commends it, and which may be easily at the first
found out by any shallow conceipt: as wee see
some fantasticke to beginne a fashion, which afterward grauity it selfe is faine to put on, because it
will not be out of the weare of other men, and
*Recti apud nos locum tenet error vbi publicus factus
est.* And power and strength that can plant itselfe
any where, hauing built within this compasse, and
reard it of so high a respect, wee now imbrace it
as the fittest dwelling for our inuention, and haue
thereon bestowed all the substance of our vnderstanding to furnish it as it is: and therefore heere
I stand foorth, onelie to make good the place we
haue thus taken vp, and to defend the sacred
monuments erected therein, which containe the
honour of the dead, the fame of the liuing, the

glory of peace, and the best power of our speach, and wherin so many honorable spirits haue sacrificed to Memorie their dearest passions, shewing by what diuine influence they haue beene moued, and vnder what starres they liued.

But yet now notwithstanding all this which I haue heere deliuered in the defence of Ryme, I am not so farre in loue with mine owne mysterie, or will seeme so froward, as to bee against the reformation, and the better setling these measures of ours. Wherein there be many things, I could wish were more certaine and better ordered, though my selfe dare not take vpon me to be a teacher therein, hauing so much neede to learne of others. And I must confesse, that to mine owne eare, those continuall cadences of couplets vsed in long and continued Poemes, are very tyresome, and vnpleasing, by reason that still, me thinks, / they runne on with a sound of one nature, and [H6 a kinde of certaintie which stuffs the delight rather then intertaines it. But yet notwithstanding, I must not out of mine owne daintinesse, condemne this kinde of writing, which peraduenture to another may seeme most delightfull, and many worthy compositions we see to haue passed with commendation in that kinde. Besides, me thinkes sometimes, to beguile the eare, with a running out, and passing ouer the Ryme, as no bound to stay vs in the line where the violence of the matter will breake thorow, is rather gracefull then otherwise. Wherein I finde my *Homer-Lucan*, as if he gloried to seeme to haue no bounds, albeit hee were confined within his measures, to be in my conceipt most happy. For so thereby, they who care not for Verse or Ryme, may passe it ouer without taking notice thereof, and please themselues with a well-measured Prose. And I must confesse my Aduersary hath wrought this much vpon me, that I thinke a Tragedie would indeede best comporte with a blank Verse, and dispence with Ryme, sauing in the *Chorus* or where a sentence shall require a couplet. And to auoyde this ouerglutting the eare with that alwayes certaine, and ful incounter of Ryme, I haue assaid in some of my Epistles to alter the vsuall place of meeting, and to sette it further off by one Verse, to trie how I could disuse my owne eare and to ease it of this continuall burthen, which indeede seemes to surcharge it a little too much, but as yet I cannot come to please my selfe therein: this alternate or crosse Ryme holding still the best place in my affection.

Besides, to me this change of number in a Poem of one nature fits not so wel, as to mixe vncertainly, feminine Rymes with masculine, which, euer since I was warned of that deformitie by my kinde friend and countriman Maister *Hugh Samford*, I haue alwayes so auoyded it, as there are not aboue two couplettes in that kinde in all my Poem of the Ciuill warres: and I would willingly if I coulde, haue altered it in all the rest, holding feminine Rymes to be fittest for Ditties, and either to be set certaine, or else by themselues. But in these things, I say, I dare not take vpon mee to teach that they ought to be so, in respect my selfe holdes them to be so, or that I thinke it right; for indeede there is no right in these things that are continually in a wandring motion, carried with the violence of our vncertaine likings, being but onely the time that giues them their power. For if this right, or truth, should be no other thing then that wee / make it, we shall shape it into a thousand [Hev figures, seeing this excellent painter Man, can so well lay the colours which himselfe grindes in his owne affections, as that hee will make them serue for any shadow, and any counterfeit. But the greatest hinderer to our proceedings, and the reformation of our errours, is th s Selfe-loue, whereunto we Versifiers are euer noted to be especially subiect; a disease of all other, the most dangerous, and incurable, being once seated in the spirits, for which there is no cure, but onely by a spirituall remedy. *Multos puto, ad sapientiam potuisse peruenire, nisi putassent se peruenisse:* and this opinion of our sufficiencie makes so great a cracke in our iudgement, as it wil hardly euer holde any thing of worth, *Cæcus amor sui,* and though it would seeme to see all without it, yet certainely it discernes but little within. For there is not the simplest writer that will euer tell himselfe, he doth ill, but as if he were the parasite onely to sooth his owne doings, perswades him that his lines can not but please others, which so much delight himselfe:

　　Suffenus est quisque sibi.　——— neque idem
　　　　vnquam.

　　AEque est beatus, ac poema cum scribit,
　　Tam gaudet in se tamque se ipse miratur.

And the more to shew that he is so, we shall see him euermore in all places, and to all persons repeating his owne compositions: and,

　　Quem vero arripuit, tenet occiditque legendo.

Next to this deformitie stands our affectation, wherein we alwayes bewray our selues to be both vn-kinde, and vnnaturall to our owne natiue language,

in disguising or forging strange or vnvsuall
wordes, as if it were to make our verse seeme an
other kind of speach out of the course of our vsuall
practise, displacing our wordes, or inuesting new,
onely vpon a singularitie: when our owne accustomed phrase, set in the due place, would expresse
vs more familiarly and to better delight, than all
this idle affectation of antiquitie, or noueltie can
euer doe. And I can not but wonder at the strange
presumption of some men that dare so audaciously
aduenture to introduce any whatsoeuer forraine
wordes, be they neuer so strange; and of themselues as it were, without a Parliament, without
any consent, or allowance, establish them as Free-
denizens in our language.   But this is but a
Character of that perpetuall reuolution which wee
see to be in all things that neuer remaine the same,
and we must heerein be content to submit our
selues to the law of time, which in few yeeres wil
make al that, for which we now contend, *Nothing*.

F I N I S.

[I1

ERRATA

The following emendations have been made in the text of the original:—

Page	Line		In the Original reads:
6	17	' powerfully '	' powerfullly '
10	9	' *arbitratores* '	' *arbritratores* '
21	14	' *Laurentius* '	' *Laurentins* '
27	10	' piller '	' piller '
42	16	' a couplet '	' a- couplet '